Monday Morning Motivational Moments ™

—Weekly Inspirations for the Heart and Soul

Linda Kedy

For Margaret
Enjoy the journey!

Linda

Monday Morning Motivational Moments
—Weekly Inspirations for the Heart and Soul

Copyright © 2003. Positive Motivational Learning, USCC. Atlanta, Georgia.

All rights reserved. Written permission must be secured from the publisher to use or reproduce any part of this book, except for brief quotations in critical reviews or articles.

Material in this book is adapted from Ms. Kedy's *Monday Morning Motivational Moments* e-zine. For more information or to subscribe, visit www.MondayMotivations.com.

To order additional copies of *Monday Morning Motivational Moments*, please go to our website at www.MondayMotivations.com

FOREWORD BY PAUL J. MEYER

Linda's journey into personal development started with one of my programs, "Dynamics of Personal Goal Setting," and she has been a student of my programs ever since.

When asked to write a testimonial for *Monday Morning Motivational Moments*, I received a draft of the book, and then felt compelled to offer to write the Foreword rather than just a testimonial.

As someone who has been in the personal development arena for over 40 years, I can spot the gems when I see them.

Monday Morning Motivational Moments is one of those gems—a new kind of book—a mix of inspirational writings and journaling opportunities.

There is a multitude of books and booklets comprising daily motivational messages, which, although they are easy to read, generally do not prompt one to take action.

True learning happens best with spaced repetition. As we repeat a process over and over again, we start to condition ourselves and find, with time, that we are applying these new principles and habits automatically.

Linda's book gives you the opportunity to review one reading every day for a week, apply the principles, and then journal the lessons that you have learned from that principle. After 52 readings you can be sure to see a major change in your attitude, beliefs, actions, and results.

—Paul J. Meyer, Founder, February 11, 2003
Success Motivation International, Inc.
Plus 40 other companies

CONTENTS

DEDICATION

In memory of my parents, the late Dr. Ernst Billig and Trude Billig, my brilliant father, who never settled for mediocrity, and my mother, who was always there for me when the going got tough—I miss you.

This book is dedicated to my two children, Marsha and Jesse, who, with their inner strength and fortitude, have inspired me more than they could ever know.

ACKNOWLEDGMENTS

With massive thanks to the following individuals who were a huge part of my inspiration to complete this project, whether they knew it or not!

My faithful MMMM readers who pestered me to put this in book form.

David Baulieu for the gift of the *One Minute Millionaire* by Mark Victor Hansen and Robert Allen (and to Mark and Robert for writing this wonderfully inspirational book).

Carol Grove, Ross Schmerse and the Date With Destiny crew for getting me moving.

Mike Litman and Bob Burg for their encouragement, guidance, and support.

Rae for her insights and beautiful cover design.

Henry for his diligent editing.

Vince for the gift of the website.

My ongoing mentors: Paul J. Meyer, Jim Rohn, Anthony Robbins, Jeff Olson, and everyone else whose seminars and trainings I have attended over the years. You have shown me that the pain of mediocrity is so much greater than the pain of growth!

Cover by: Rae Jensan

Edited by: Henry Brent and Rae Jensan

Designed by: Jennifer Wewers

Website by: Vince Petrell

Inspired by my faithful readers—bless you for your never-ending support!

INTRODUCTION

According to Stephen Covey, there are four stages of competence that apply in every area of life, especially in the field of personal development:

1. We don't know that we need to grow (unconscious incompetence)
2. We feel the need to start working on ourselves (conscious incompetence)
3. Total focus on self, feeling the pain of growth (conscious competence)
4. A time of gratitude and giving back (unconscious competence)

In 1997, after being stuck in "working on myself" personal development programs for five years, I realized the time had come to broaden my horizons, quit focusing on just me, and start contributing and bringing value to others! Being determined to continue growing (and needing to feel the pain), I chose to contribute in an area that was way out of my comfort zone—my worst subject in school—creative writing.

The first writing was created on a Sunday night and emailed to some friends on a Monday morning. The response was "motivating" and so Monday Morning Motivational Moments was born. Over the next four years my friends started forwarding the writings to their friends around the world and requests to subscribe would come in from different continents. My database of readers grew and grew. Whenever I had a tough time getting inspired and would consider quitting the writings, my readers would get upset.

Many of my readers asked me when "the book" would be published—at the time, that was the furthest thing from my mind. Then they challenged me—and I accepted the challenge! Thus began a remarkable journey of creation, which I now share with you.

Enjoy.

Linda

Monday
Morning
Motivational
Moments

—Weekly Inspirations for the Heart and Soul

A series of weekly inspirational readings designed to encourage you to look at life from different perspectives.

On Accountability

Accountability, personal integrity, character—we have many different names for this concept, but really it's all about personal responsibility in relationships.

Recently I read, "One trouble with the world is that so many people who stand up for their rights fall down on their duties."

How busy we get trying to take care of other people's accountability, and how eloquent we can be as we preach to them about integrity. But what about ourselves?

Kindness has influenced far more people than eloquence, yet this is the dilemma:

- Are we really kinder by not holding people accountable, or does this just endorse their behavior and enable them to continue their lack of accountability?
- If our expectations of others are unfulfilled do we not often end up in judgment of them?
- Once we establish our standards are vastly different than others, should we just move on from these relationships?

We can avoid all conflict by having no expectations, yet we then often find ourselves compromising our own integrity.

The bottom line is that if we celebrate our similarities, rather than curse our differences, within all our relationships, we can continually do as Elizabeth Barret Browning suggests and "Light up tomorrow with today."

Let's worry less about what others do and say, take care of our own responsibilities, and our reputations will take care of themselves.

In the words of that beautiful spiritual song, we have all been lost and blind, but with the "Amazing Grace" of God, we can be found, and we can see.

What I've learned...

On Celebrating Change

As we move forward from a century of incredible change, we must wonder what comes next:

- A century where transportation went from horse and buggy to motor vehicles and spaceships—where we can get to the moon faster than we used to be able to cross one state.
- A century where communication went from penning a letter for hand delivery, to remote email—where we can communicate with thousands of people faster than we used to be able to pen one sentence.
- A century where industries were created and wealth was built from the ground up, to e-commerce—where it becomes faster to IPO a dot.com company than it used to be to draw up a business plan for a conventional business.

As we reflect on the years since our respective births (for some of us that means a long memory!), much has changed—yet so much remains unchanged.

As I listen to the Bible reading of a child born in a manger, I remember in elementary school listening to the Christmas service in a beautiful old church in England. Nothing has changed.

Five years ago I celebrated Christmas Eve in Bethlehem. Today the city is "closed for the holidays" because of the violence in the area.

If we can move, communicate, and create massive wealth so quickly, should we not also be able to create our well-being quickly?

The biggest transition this century was a change in the value system of the modern world—from love, nurturing, and family to the "quick fix" syndrome, business and wealth beats family and health.

What we must come back to is love, for ourselves and for one another, because only when you love yourself can others truly love you. And only when you love yourself can you truly love others.

In the words of Albert Pine, "What we do for ourselves dies with us—what we do for others remains and is immortal."

What I've learned...

On Balance Sheets

Now is the time to check out your bank accounts, both the financial ones as well as the relationship ones. Stephen Covey teaches that in order to make withdrawals, we must first make deposits.

Deposits can be in so many different ways: a smile, a phone call, a card, a gift, a hug, fulfillment of a promise, listening, nurturing, truly caring, etc.

Withdrawals are also varied—sometimes we plan them with a request for help or support, but usually they are involuntary, such as: a harsh look, a harsh word, a no-show, non-fulfillment of a promise, and conscious or even unconscious uncaring.

First, check out the financial balance sheet, the income versus expenses, as well as the assets versus liabilities. Then, become clear on how you will successfully manage your finances from this day forth.

Next, check out the emotional balance sheet:
- Income (who/what contributes to our emotional well-being)
- Expenses (who/what consistently drains us emotionally)
- Assets (long-term relationships that we wish to hold on to)
- Liabilities (relationships that we need to sever for our long term well-being)

It's time to draw up your own balance sheets and commit to keeping positive balances in your accounts.

Although the big picture may be healthy overall because of some massive deposits that you or others may be putting into your account, your individual accounts with some people may be way off balance—either you have been irresponsible enough to take out huge loans or have given huge loans without collateral.

It's time to re-evaluate every account, wipe the slate clean, and commit to putting in more than you can ever hope to withdraw!

What I've learned...

On Goal Setting

So how was your week?

Did you get on track, set your goals, create your treasure map, get busy, and start the activities that will lead you in the direction of your desires and your dreams?

Did you get focused, get committed to your project for the year, get passionate about your life and share your passion with others?

Did you workout, spend some time nurturing yourself, read a good educational book, say your prayers, contemplate who you can help and support?

Did you experience the happiness of being busy and directed, the sincerity of your communications, the pride of starting the week/month/year/millennium on track?

Or did you mess up already, break some of your own rules, eat the wrong food, skip your workout, procrastinate over those phone calls, spend too much time browsing the Internet, forget to call the family, delete emails you should have answered, or get impatient with your loved ones?

Guess what?

Today is the first day of the rest of your life. You get to forgive yourself, get a second chance to start over.

But this week, this time, please get serious and get going!

Some of us are so self-forgiving, so often, that we can end up hardly moving forward at all.

Then again, some of us are so self-critical and unforgiving that we forget to acknowledge ourselves for our achievements, constantly comparing ourselves with others.

Consider carefully what is really important to you, the immediate achievements (and accolades that go with them), sometimes representing only temporary success, or the strong foundation where recognition may not be immediate, but long-term success is guaranteed.

Whatever is right for you may not be right for those around you, so just remember at all times the Platinum Rule (versus the Golden Rule): Do unto others as they would like to be "done unto" (versus "do unto others as you would have them do unto you").

In other words, give people what they wish to receive, rather than what you wish to give them, and you'll find yourself receiving all you can dream of!

What I've learned...

On Habits

Every week, for over two years, I wrote my "Monday Morning Motivational Moments," yet in just two weeks, I created the habit of not writing.

Every day, for over three years, I checked and responded to email several times a day, yet in just ten days without access to a computer I created the habit of not doing email.

Several times a week, for many years, I worked out at the gym, and in just a couple of weeks I created the habit of not working out.

Bad habits are so easy to pick up and so hard to break. On the other hand, great habits are so hard to pick up and yet so easy to break!

In the words of the great General H. Norman Schwarzkopf, "The hard part is doing it." And the easiest thing of all is justifying not doing the right thing (I'm sure you don't do this, but you probably know someone who does!). Maybe there was a shift in priorities, health factors, out-of-town travel, high-tech goes low-tech, or all of the above.

So, instead of giving you all my justifications, today I am making it a MUST to recreate the great habits and reframe the bad ones.

This is the only way to continue onwards and upwards; the journey may be tough (writing this was really tough), yet the satisfaction of having done it far outweighs the pain of procrastination.

So, quoting two of our most inspiring motivators: "We MUST learn how to be happy with what we have while we pursue all that we want" (Jim Rohn), and "When someone does something well, applaud! You will make two people happy" (Samuel Goldwyn).

Applaud me, the writing is writ, and I'm to the gym!

How about you? What will you make a MUST this week?

On Confusion

So much in our world seems to be turned around! We turn our home offices into high-tech efficiency, then spend hours on hold with hi-tech companies' low-tech customer service personnel.

We shop efficiently online with companies that draft payment from our accounts instantaneously, then spend ages searching for customer service information, which is often secreted away somewhere on the website in the hope that we won't track them down!

Customer service should be something we love; today it's something we get to endure, with anything from "Sorry, there's just nothing that can be done," to "The supervisor doesn't work today". The ultimate pain is when you've finally gotten through to the person who actually can help...and the call gets disconnected!

Every now and again we come across an absolute gem, someone who genuinely wants to resolve our issues quickly and efficiently, someone who goes way and above the call of duty and makes us feel good in the process.

Let's all commit to acknowledging these rare and wonderful people, whenever and wherever we meet them. Let them know just how much they are truly appreciated.

We could always just look at the George Carlin Theory About Life
> The most unfair thing about life is the way it ends. I mean, life is tough. It takes up a lot of your time. What do you get at the end of it? Death. What's that, a bonus? I think the life cycle is all backwards. You should die first, get it out of the way. Then you live in an old age home. You get kicked out when you're too young, get a gold watch and go to work. You work 40 years until you're young enough to enjoy   your retirement. You do drugs, alcohol, you party, and you get ready for high school. You go to grade school, you become a kid, you play, you have no responsibilities. You become a little baby, you go back into the womb, spend your last nine months floating...and you finish off as an orgasm!

What a concept!

What I've learned...

On Love

What a dilemma! I'm unsure whether to write about love or money (as opposed to the love of money).

Valentine's Day is the obvious love factor, and my company giving unprecedented huge cash bonuses was the surprise money factor.

Oh, Valentine's Day—that interesting time of year that means little to some people, more to others, and for some, it can be the "be all and end all" of a relationship.

What is most important on this day, as on anniversaries, birthdays, and other special days, is not only getting what you want, but ensuring your partner gets what he or she wants (rather than what you want to give).

Did you show your loved ones in some little way how much you really care? Or did you put your heart on the line and say what you meant even if you knew the feelings may not be reciprocated? Did you read the story "The Rose" about the husband who set up advance delivery for red roses to his wife for as long as she lived, even after he passed on?

We have to do it—we must put the love out there, no matter what.

In the words of the late Mother Theresa, "The hunger for love is much more difficult to remove than the hunger for bread."

There is no right or wrong way to express your love if it truly comes from the heart. In fact, there's no right or wrong way for anything, so long as we don't intentionally cause pain.

I love to read the writings of Rumi who says, "Out beyond ideas of right thinking or wrong thinking there is a field. I'll meet you there."

And my favorite, which I'll leave you with as a great credo for life, "Work like you don't need the money. Love like you've never been hurt. Dance like nobody's watching."

What I've learned...

On Angels

Once upon a time there was a child ready to be born. The child asked God, "They tell me you are sending me to earth tomorrow, but how am I going to live there being so small and helpless?"

God replied, "Among the many angels, I chose one for you. Your angel will be waiting for you and will take care of you."

The child further inquired, "But tell me, here in heaven I don't have to do anything but sing and smile and be happy."

God said, "Your angel will sing for you and will also smile for you everyday. And you will feel your angel's love and be very happy."

Again the child asked, "And how am I going to be able to understand when people talk to me if I don't know the language?"

God said, "Your angel will tell you the most beautiful and sweet words you will ever hear, and with much patience and care, your angel will teach you how to speak."

"And what am I going to do when I want to talk to you?"

God said, "Your angel will place your hands together and will teach you how to pray."

"I've heard that on earth there are bad men. Who will protect me."

God said, "Your angel will defend you even if it means risking its life."

"But I will always be sad because I will not see you anymore."

God said, "Your angel will always talk to you about me and will teach you the way to come back to me, even thought I will always be next to you."

At that moment there was much peace in heaven, but voices from earth could be heard and the child hurriedly asked, "God, if I am to leave now, please tell me my angel's name."

"Her name is not important. You will simply call her 'Mom.'"
—Author Unknown

On Tests

Have you ever felt you're being tested?

My commitment this week, stated clearly and daily in my agenda, was "stay focused, no matter what." I guess God wanted to see if I was serious, so I got some true tests:

- A week of no water in the house,
- extra financial obligations showing up,
- financial commitments from others not fulfilled,
- losing my laptop for two weeks while it was repaired,
- having it restored to factory conditions (with no data left on it),
- losing my complete time/project/contact management system, and, of course,
- having several conflicting appointments (as I couldn't recall what was already booked)!

So, how was your week?

Thank you God, for the opportunity to make me stronger, and especially for my Pre-Paid Legal service!

Strangely enough, my "stay focused, no matter what" note is what got me through the week and resulted in me writing more business this week than I usually write in a month.

Asking great questions such as "what's really happening here?" also helped. After the database wipeout, I got an email from a friend suggesting this may be an opportunity to make a "fresh start?" There were two responses that I could have chosen—one was unprintable(!) and the second was "you bet—this is a fresh start!"

All the hundreds of wonderful friends who emailed me their information gave me permission to stay in touch, and the few "unsubscribes" were a great way to clean out old contacts.

What would happen if you lost your contact base or daytimer? Would you grieve or start over with a fresh new attitude and true friends?

Try it, you could like it!

What I've learned...

On Learning

"We are drowning in information, yet we are starving for wisdom," says Anthony Robbins.

Information overload is definitely kicking in. When I reflect on what I have read and learned just during the last month, it is pretty amazing.

I read hundreds of emails questioning the September 11th tragedy from every perspective: opinions as to why America is loved, why America is hated, etc.

A great question was apparently asked on a Philly radio call-in show: Given two highly influential men—one develops relatively cheap software for the world and gives hundreds of millions of dollars to charities, the other sponsors terrorism and causes massive death and destruction, "Why is it that the US government has spent more money chasing down Bill Gates over the past ten years than Osama bin Laden?"

However, the one underlying request in virtually every message was a call (and dozens of petitions) for peace.

I learned several great new health-related technologies, as well as some very ancient ones, including the healing powers of organic living and raw foods, healing through detoxification of the lymphatic system, and balancing the body energetically.

I learned to take an individual sales presentation and turn it into a group presentation, and receive group gratitude (even bigger than individual gratitude!). I found that when we have the right audience, location is not important—construction sites, car-parks, gas stations are a great!

I experienced the pleasures of being a property owner: figuring out how to fix the mower, mow the lawn, create a vegetable garden, chase hornets out of the house, avoid huge spiders and their webs, reseal garage doors, and, I'm sure, many more novel experiences at my Sanctuary.

I realize that, had I had this knowledge sooner, I may have had the wisdom to make different decisions. Then I remember that everything we learn is learned at exactly the right time—God's timing is always perfect.

So, what have you learned recently? Document it, acknowledge the lesson, and get ready for the next one!

What I've learned...

On Financial Empowerment

When we feel financially challenged, what are our options?

- Go into scarcity mode, panic, and convince ourselves that there will never be enough,
- Tell ourselves that we're not smart enough to get out of the rut, or really worthy of being wealthy,
- Look, at what caused us to run out of money, borrow some and go and do more of that behavior,
- Find a way to get stuff for free, talk our way into events and meals and bum off our friends and family,
- Borrow a little bit from a lot of people, and a lot from a handful of people, then pay back the little bits, so lots of people think we're great, and only a handful will disagree.

OR

- Check our pockets and make a conscious effort to write down exactly where we are spending every penny,
- Find a great cause to give to, knowing that by giving we are making room to receive,
- Check our self-esteem to see if we really do feel worthy,
- Check our philosophy to see if we're practicing poor habits or wealthy habits (the rich invest their money and spend what is left; the poor spend their money and invest what's left),
- Check our plan, if we have one, to see if we really are on the right track and in the right place at the right time,
- Check our efforts to see if we are really taking the actions that will produce the results we desire.

The best option, after checking that our plans are well directed, is to ensure our energies are being used where they will create results, not just potential results, especially if we are commission based. Marketing is important, but sales are what pay!

Pay attention to what works and what doesn't, get better at what we do by doing more of it; the more we do, the better we become and the results will follow.

On The Book of Life

I recently heard a wonderful talk called, "Write Your Life."

The concept of this talk brought home how the different periods of our lives are just chapters in our own personal novels, or, for some of us, our own personal soap operas!

Characters appear for a while, fulfill their missions, and then disappear from the soaps or the book. One chapter or episode may be dedicated to your early childhood or your teenage escapades; another may cover a period of sickness; yet another may cover an unnecessary business venture or a huge windfall, or maybe successful participation in a beauty pageant (Did you see Sandra Bullock in *Miss Congeniality*?).

When we use this analogy, it no longer becomes strange why some people show up in our lives and move on, whilst others come in and out for decades during the duration of our life novels.

How often do you re-read your old chapters?

Do you re-read the ones that made you laugh or the ones that created sorrow?

Do you get so stuck in an old chapter that you have no motivation to write a new one?

What chapter are you writing right now?

Have you had to write some characters or habits out of your life?

I trust you are writing some great new habits and people into your life!

Looked at in this way—every chapter is nothing more than a new personal goal, and every goal is nothing more than another episode in your life.

Every episode will have a different focus: sometimes business, sometimes health, sometimes family, sometimes spirituality—always depending on the current priorities in your life.

Just be sure and remember that your life is just that, YOUR life, and you have the God-given ability to write it any way that you choose!

Let's begin our new chapter today, and make sure that we write the positive ending first!

What I've learned...

33

On Miracles

Miracles do happen!

After being diagnosed with breast cancer, I made a fairly last-minute decision to attend Anthony Robbins "Date With Destiny" in Palm Springs, CA. My outcomes were very clear:

- To contribute to the participants at the same time as totally nurturing myself,
- To fully heal my body by getting to the absolute root of the cause of the disease I was carrying,
- To connect with healers and practitioners of alternative methods
- to place myself in an environment where 90% of people have first hand knowledge of self-cure versus the 95% in my regular environment suggesting more drastic measures.

In those ten days I met many of my angels, some in human form and others in a form invisible to the human eye. I reconnected with the angles who had been with me since birth, those same angels I rejected 30 years ago. I became aware of the dramas I had created in my life for those last 30 years and how effortless my life would have been had I acknowledged them!

Miracles do happen—every day!

All we need to do is feel worthy of receiving them (self-love), be grateful for them even before they happen (gratitude), expect them daily (anticipation), and laugh about the ease with which they show up (humor) When we commit to experiencing these emotions, consciously, every day, we cannot help but attract miracles. When we are clear on our intentions and the outcome we desire (goal-setting), it makes it so much easier for our miracle worker (God) to bring us our gifts.

Are you ready for yours—are you really ready?

Try it out for size—read *Absolute Effortless Prosperity* by Bijan. Do the simple daily assignments and just be sure you're ready for the abundance of miracles and gifts that will show up for you.

What I've learned...

On Peacefulness

Peace or turmoil—that is the question.

Whatever the question, whenever you need to make a decision, by all means weigh the pros and cons and when that's done, go inside yourself and see how that decision resonates for you—does it bring you peace or turmoil?

Recently, I had some very difficult decisions to make—some relating to my health, some to my family, and some to my business. Every time I felt overwhelmed, I returned back to the true question: peace or turmoil? And God guided me back to peace.

This week, I rejected drama and replaced it with peace; I rejected pressure and replaced it with peace; I rejected fear and replaced it with peace.

Sometimes peace can come from meditation (Kitaro's music is awesome for that); sometimes projecting waves of love onto an angry person can diffuse the anger and bring peace; sometimes just thinking of something really funny and laughing out loud can diffuse tension and bring peace.

I encourage you to experiment with this: try staying tense and see what drama you can attract. Alternatively, commit to being peaceful, no matter what, and you will be amazed at the wonderful events and people that will be attracted to you.

And if you don't laugh enough (laughter is the best healer), then buy yourself a book of jokes and start your week on a great track!

On Opportunity

Another birthday already? What's up with that?

These birthdays used to come once a year and we'd spend months anticipating them. Now they pop around every couple of months when we're not looking!

Every year brings many changes in our lives, and, depending on our outlook on life, these can be great challenges or great celebrations.

Focus on abundance and gratitude and you'll always celebrate; focus on ego and scarcity and you'll always have new challenges.

So often we look at the changes in our lives as a loss instead of the opportunity that they really represent—the only time we miss the opportunity is when our faith is weak.

> When we walk to the edge of all the light we have and take the step into the darkness of the unknown, we must believe that one of two things will happen: there will be something solid for us to stand on or we will be taught to fly. (Patrick Overton)

Do this exercise for just one week: for every apparent loss or challenge, search for the gain or opportunity and write it down. Journal it. By the end of one week you will be amazed at the apparent miracles that have shown up for you just because you changed your perception.

There are enough miracles for us all if we just pay attention. I wish each and every one of you enough in your own lives.

> I wish you enough sun to keep your attitude bright. I wish you enough rain to appreciate the sun more. I wish you enough happiness to keep your spirit alive. I wish you enough pain to satisfy your wanting. I wish you enough loss to appreciate all that you possess. I wish you enough "Hello's" to get you through the final "Goodbye." *–Anon*

What I've learned...

On Reconciliation

Recently I started to understand some of the profound intricacies revolving around relationships, both in the personal and business realms.

What became clear is how much we do to avoid healing relationships. Especially when we feel we've done all we can and now it's "their turn."

Whether it's a personal friend or family member we want to love or mentor, or a client we want to do business with, we must have the ability to influence them:

- To influence, we must have a solid relationship.
- To create a relationship we must first reconcile differences.
- To reconcile differences we must establish trust with that person.
- To establish trust, we must make it safe for the other person to communicate with us.
- To make it safe, we must be humble and not defend ourselves.

When we defend ourselves and make a point about being right, that makes the other person wrong.

When we have no defense, we let them know how much we value them.

But how do we accept someone when we dislike their behavior or lifestyle?

How do we forgive someone when their behavior has hurt or offended us?

Is it more important to be offended by their behavior or to heal the relationship?

Is it more important for us to make a point or to make a friend?

How often should you try to reconcile a relationship when previous efforts have been in vain?

The answer is "as long as it takes," especially if this is a family member or long-time friend.

Give everything that you can give, whenever you can give it, and you'll be amazed, as I have been, at the incredible friends that show up in your life when you most need them!

In the words of the Arab proverb, "If you have much, give of your wealth; if you have little, give of your heart."

___

What I've learned...

On Thanks

After a five-hour surgery, at least 30 inches of incisions (and a beautifully reconstructed body...hee hee!), it is absolutely amazing, after just two days, to be home, walking around, up and down stairs and totally pain free.

Thanks to the grace of God, the power of Prayer, and the power of friendship—what a miraculous combination.

For your brilliant works of art, thank you to my surgeons, Dr. Cowgill and Dr. Beegle.

For all my wonderful nurses, whose names I can't recall (every time I learned your names, your shifts changed!)—thank you.

For the beautiful bouquets of flowers that filled my room and the hallway (and had everyone's allergies going!), thank you, especially Paul J. Meyer and family and the Tony Robbins crew.

For the surprise gift boxes, food, and juices (that got the nurses asking about healthy nutritional habits!) to nourish my soul and body—thank you.

For your wonderful company (even when I was too zoned out to be coherent)—thank you.

For your patience in calling to check on me (and calling back again and again until the line was free!)—thank you.

For your beautiful and comical cards (some of which stretched my stitches laughing!)—thank you.

For your generous time and guidance—thank you to all my "alternative" (natural) healers.

For staying with me the night before surgery and for bringing me safely home—thank you.

For everyone who wrote business while I was unable to, and created those wonderful override commissions for me—thank you.

If I forgot you, this is a great opportunity for you to practice forgiveness!

If your name isn't here and you prayed for me, I love you and bless you!

If your name isn't here and you didn't think of me, I love you anyway!

What I've learned...

On Healing

The healing process is absolutely fascinating.

Our body has an innate ability to heal trauma at extraordinary speed. Our mind, however, will keep our traumatic memories around forever if we allow it!

Preparation, or sharpening the axe, is what truly makes the difference in healing. Physical preparation, be it for surgery or an unexpected trauma, means keeping your body cleansed—with regular digestive tract cleanses and parasite cleanses (yes, we all have parasites!). It means strengthening your immune system, cleansing the organs of your body, especially your liver and kidneys, cooling your blood and keeping your body nourished and hydrated, removing from your diet: sugar, saturated fats, caffeine, and artificial preservatives and coloring.

Make this your normal way of living, minimizing the toxins from cosmetics, cleaning products, and pollution, and your body will reject disease.

Mental preparation is not as simple, yet it is very achievable. It means keeping your mind cleansed of negative thoughts, fear, anger, scarcity, jealousy; and strengthening your emotions of love, gratitude, anticipation, and passion. When you cleanse the deepest recesses of your mind from any historical thoughts that no longer serve you, you look at every moment for what is great in your life right now. It means paying attention to whose presence brings you peace versus who brings you stress, whose energy builds you up versus who drains your energy. It means letting go of resentment and remembering that, in the words of Gandhi, "An eye for an eye only ends up making the whole world blind." Buddha said, "Anger will never disappear so long as thoughts of resentment are cherished in the mind. Anger will disappear just as soon as thoughts of resentment are forgotten."

Make yourself a promise always to do more than the bare minimum. Give more than people expect of you, and your rewards will be multiplied tremendously.

Let me share with you the candle of love, hope, and friendship that came to me this week: "I asked God for water, He gave me an ocean. I asked God for a flower, He gave me a garden. I asked God for a tree, He ve me a forest. I asked God for a friend, and He gave me you. There is t enough darkness in the world to put out the light of this one candle."

hat I've learned...

On Mothers

Mother's Day!

Moms are excitedly answering the doorbell, receiving unexpected cards, bouquets of flowers, resting in bed while breakfast arrives on a tray, getting surprise visits from their loving children, hearing the phone ring off the hook with well wishes from their kids, phone-calls and surprise visits from surrogate children...or are they?

If your Mom is still living, have you called her today?

Mother's Day is celebrated at different times in different parts of the world and those of us with children overseas could be disappointed if the children didn't remember this date. Fortunately we have wonderful friends in the US who are remembering us.

However, have you included all the "moms" in your life? In this time of multiple marriages and extended families, this may take a little more effort than it used to.

Here are some of the people you should be remembering:

- For all of us, our moms (of course) and grandmothers. For those of us whose moms have passed on, this is a great time to communicate with them in spirit—and to know they will be receiving our love and blessings.
- For those of us who are or have been married, our mothers-in-law and/or ex mothers-in-law.
- For those of us who are step-parents, our step-children's moms.
- For those of us who, for whatever sad reason, are not in touch with our moms, our surrogate moms.
- For those of us who are in relationship, date, or have friends who are single moms, this would be a great time to recognize them in motherhood.

So, guys and gals, we moms are so excited and waiting in anticipation with bated breath for the wonderful magic moments we know you will create for us today!

On Associations

"We become the average of the people we spend the most time with." I've heard this before many times, but I only just really "got it."

Try this exercise for one week and analyze the results:

- Step #1—Jot down the names of the people you speak to and the length of the call or meeting. At the end of the week, total up the number of minutes/hours you spent in conversation with each person.
- Step #2—being totally truthful, grade each one of these people on a scale of 1-10 based on how much they not only support you, but also empower you to be the best you can be.
- Step #3—think of people that you know, or would like to get to know, who always encourage and support you unconditionally—how much time are you spending with them, in person or in conversation?

So what have you been choosing for yourself...and what are you committed to choosing in the future?

You can always choose to spend more time with those who empower you...so long as you are also on their list of empowering people

Be committed to hanging out only in places where you feel good– you'll find the people around you will either adapt to your well-being so that you can start enjoying one another's company or they will quietly move-on and be less present in your day to day life.

On Adversity

In every adversity there is a seed of opportunity—did you plant a lot of seeds over the last 12 months?

Just get excited about which of these adversity seeds are going to sprout next year, and the fruit and blessings that will come from them.

Reframing situations (looking at the positive in a negative situation) is one of the most valuable skills we can learn. When "life" kicks in, over and over and over and over again, it's imperative to keep focused on the eye of the storm, which is always calm.

It's also during the times of adversity that we really recognize who is there to support us versus those who just stick around to judge. Many of us have much healing to do in our personal and business relationships, and often we try to heal a relationship before the other party is ready.

I bless the friend who reminded me that each one of us is 100% responsible for 50% of our relationships.

We have often heard that we can choose our friends but we can't choose our families, so many of us have created extended "families" through our friends.

Yet the truth is that God chose our families for us and, if we do not nurture our blood relationships, then we are disrespecting God's wishes.

So let's give 100% in every relationship and let the other party do their part, if and when they are ready.

On Rules

Needs, values, rules—we all have them and they are different for each of us.

Hardly surprising then that one out of two marriages in this country fail. What if there was a way to get really clear on your needs and what you value most?

What if there was a way to discover your rules for happiness?

Best of all, what if there was a way to quickly identify these in a potential partner, or better still, in your current partner?

The good news is that you can do it on a first date, especially if it's a "date with destiny."

This week I had the best date of my life—a "date with destiny" with over one thousand people from thirty countries!

It was amazing to find that almost everyone really wants the same thing—to love, to be happy, and to contribute.

Also, almost everyone has one of the same two or three hang-ups.

It's our personal rules that we need to look at—our rules for feeling love and happiness, or feeling bad.

Most of us have loads of ways to feel bad and very few to feel great.

Fortunately, we can change our rules—we can make it easy to feel pleasure and hard to feel pain.

We can ask empowering questions. Instead of the "Why me?" I had been asking, my question became, "How can I best be a shining example of love and light, celebrating an extraordinary life, whilst creating a multitude of magical moments for myself and others?"

Try to identify the question that rules your life (we all have one, and it usually starts with "Why can't I...").

Then, come up with your new empowering question—ask it at every opportunity and see how extraordinary your life can instantly become!

On Negativity

It only takes a little drop of dirt to make pure water murky, and it only takes a small shadow to make a bright light dim.

There is so much negativity in our world, criticism, bad news, even in our Olympics there was more attention given to the negative judging than to the amazing performances! The question is, "How much is each of us contributing to this negative energy?"

Have you noticed how, when we have even the smallest issue, we tend to create a story, make it a drama, and tell the story over and over and over again. What would happen if we caught ourselves doing this and refused to talk about the drama?

When someone asks what happened, tell them a joke instead!

Have you noticed how easy it is to find fault with people (don't bother to congratulate yourself for finding faults—that's easy, anyone can do it!), yet sometimes we have to dig very deep to find their treasures.

What would happen if we forced ourselves only to look for the treasure and only to talk about others in a complimentary way?

Try this for size—if someone ignores or offends you, make them your target of love and don't let up until they get it!

Make a true effort this week to get just 1/3 of one percent better every day and in a year you'll be twice as good!

Helen Keller said it best, "Keep your face to the sunshine and you cannot see the shadows."

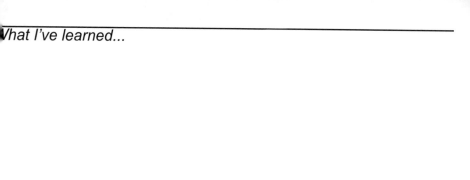

What I've learned...

On Letting Go

Fix it now, or let it go, but do something!

Apathy or procrastination will eventually produce alienation from the beauty of life. There is a fine line between taking action in the direction of resolution and, when resolution evades us, being aware that continued action will just drain us.

That fine line is intelligence!

How much time and energy we expend on issues that cannot be resolved. Sometimes, especially when it's a matter of principle (i.e. it violates our values), we have the hardest time letting go.

Sometimes we just need to let go of issues that are haunting us, even if we have no idea how these issues will be taken care of. The recognition that other people's responsibilities are just that, their responsibilities, is huge.

The peace that comes from letting go is amazing. As you refocus your energy on the positive, it will open up space for you to tap into your creativity, to allow wonderful new people into your life, and so much more!

Such insights create great joy, yet we must realize that these gifts are of no true value until they are shared or ministered—and that's why I continue to commit to writing, every week!

Are you sharing your precious gifts?

What I've learned...

On Leadership

What a party we had—celebrating with ten thousand colleagues our company's 30-year anniversary!

Our impressive keynote speakers included Attorney Generals (current and prior), the Lieutenant Governor, and one of my all-time favorites from Atlanta, John Addison, the Co-CEO of Primerica, who shared some wonderful points on leadership.

Mr. Addison is a unique speaker, with a colorful vocabulary, who always has a unique message to encourage us to look at our strengths and weaknesses:

- All great leaders are inspirers, not intimidators—what is your methodology for helping your friends and colleagues in their development?
- Leaders have the mentality of a humble servant—are you living life humbly or waiting for it to humble you?
- Always keep a winning attitude—are you continually feeding (envisioning) your dreams just or focusing on your nightmares?
- Create a winning environment, one of competition, non-judgment, fun, and inclusivity—are you inclusive or exclusive with all members of your team and your support group?
- Respond to adversity—when adversity hits, do you choose to get better or get bitter, respond or react?

Winning is voluntary. Have you ever wondered why so many people don't, won't, or think they can't win, because they didn't realize it was just a matter of choice, not chance?

As leaders in our businesses, our families or our communities, there are plenty of opportunities to get frustrated, especially when we see potential in others that they are having difficulty seeing in themselves, or when we know that a simple methodology will work, yet others are certai they must complicate it!

Whenever you are unsure how to deal with someone, choose love over anger. As Bernie Siegel says so beautifully, "An overdose of love has no recorded adverse side-effects!"

On Interpretation

So what really happened?

If someone ignores you, do you instantly feel rejected, or do you consider the fact that they may not have heard your request or were pre-occupied or just plain didn't know how to deal with your request?

Often I have been called to support friends who were upset because of the way they had interpreted certain incidents.

The challenge was not so much what happened as it was the meaning that they gave to the incident.

When we have a confrontation with someone, is it about them and their issues, or could it possibly be about us?

Maybe we recognize a trait in them that causes us to get defensive because it's a trait that we dislike in ourselves.

Maybe the confrontation will be uncomfortable enough that it becomes a catalyst for both parties to change.

Whenever these situations come up, the first place to look is in the mirror. Ask the question, "So what really happened? Is there any way that I could have handled this differently?"

We can always improve our behaviors, especially if we remember the Platinum Rule, "Do unto others as they would be done unto." This means nothing more than, instead of giving people what you would want to receive if you were in their situation, giving them what they want (i.e. instead of giving them what you hallucinate that they want, learn how to recognize and fill others' actual needs).

How often have we found it easy to forgive ourselves (for messing up, procrastinating, etc.), yet been frustrated with others because they did not handle a situation perfectly (they messed up, procrastinated, etc.).

As we learn, others will learn. As we grow, others will grow. As we forgive ourselves, others will forgive themselves.

It all starts with the person in the mirror.

Check your mirror and bless yourself today and every day!

What I've learned...

On Seasons

In Atlanta we often have all four seasons in one week:
- 70 degrees on Sunday—summer is on the way!
- Pine cones falling off the trees—I guess it's still fall!
- Below freezing at night—it's still winter!
- Daffodils blooming—I guess it's spring!

Jim Rohn always talks of the seasons of life (they just seemed to come around a little faster this week).

The truth is that day always follows night, and, though the night may seem long, it's never more than a few hours.

Fall always follows summer, which follows spring, which follows winter, and, though the seasons may seem long, they are never more than few months.

It can just seem longer if you are a thermometer (only reacting to outside forces), yet time can fly by if you are a thermostat (only reacting to your inner forces).

The only two things we can really change are our responses to what happens, and our anticipation of what will happen.

Get upset by an issue or a person and anticipate that they are out to get you, and you can live a miserable life. Respond to a person by realizing that they are great—they merely displayed poor behavior—and anticipate that they will bring huge value to your life in the future, and you can live in daily bliss!

Never let anyone withdraw from your (emotional) bank account...and don't withdraw from theirs.

Trust that things will work out for the best and be committed to showing up at your best. Pay attention to what shows up in your life—sometimes we're so busy with our daily activities that we miss, or forget, to cherish the special times.

If you really want to bring value to someone's life, whether personally or in the field of sales, stop doing an analysis of their needs and start analyzing their desires. This way you'll be focusing on "opening" new relationships and you'll never have to close a sale again!

On Weeding

It's so easy to start a job and leave it half-finished.

How many times do we start something, almost finish it, then get distracted or tired or else start to justify that we've made such good progress that it's all right to quit.

Starting a long overdue project does give some real satisfaction, but that does not nearly compare with the satisfaction of completing it. Some projects can seem so large that they are really overwhelming—the key is to chunk them into smaller tasks.

I started a project one beautiful Sunday—weeding the yard. My beautiful sanctuary has the hugest, most beautiful yard I have ever owned and the thought of weeding it seemed quite overwhelming.

So, I chunked it down, took a couple of small sections of the front yard, nearly quit a few times, persisted, and got it done...yeah!

Weeding always reminds me of an article I wrote several years ago. When the weeds are young, they are easy to remove. If we ignore them and let them grow, the root structure gets stronger and stronger and becomes more difficult to remove. If we continue to ignore them, they will take over the garden. These are the laws of nature and they apply in every area of living within the plant and animal kingdoms.

So beware of the weeds in your personal life (neglected health principles) and in your family life (neglected nurturing of relationships), and in your financial life (neglected learning of financial principles), and in your nation's life (neglected terrorism).

Pay attention to what is happening around you, even if it may not seem relevant at that time, because one weed, unheeded, can kill your flowers as well as your garden and create massive destruction. Weed your garden as you go, weed regularly, and let the flowers in your life bloom to their heart's content.

hat I've learned...

On Focus

Where are you choosing to focus?

Today I choose to focus peacefully on the act of prayer, the fun an health benefits of dance, any excuse to laugh, the expectation of huge income, and the anticipation of spending some glorious time with my son

We are the only species that has the ability to really make choices versus simply following our animal instincts, yet the choices we make are often not those that move us forward in life. It's time to become more aware of the choices available and the effects that they have on our joy and well-being:

- Should we focus on making things happen or choose peace and allow things to happen?
- Should we focus on having people do the right thing or choose peace and know that what we think is right might not be right for them?
- Should we focus on looking for huge results or choose peace and acknowledge every little gift and every precious moment spent with those dear to us?
- Should we focus on the somewhat distorted reports as to who is terrorizing whom in the Middle East or choose peace and know that peace will come soon for all God's chosen people?
- Should we focus on taking serious action to collect from our debtors or choose peace and trust that these people wi take care of their obligations or reap the consequences?
- Should we focus on the seriousness and intensity of today' political situations or choose peace and look for every excuse to laugh, sing, and dance?

Choose your focus well this week, and always.

What I've learned...

On Compromise

How often do you compromise?

If it's just as important to do the right thing as it is to do things right, why do we compromise?

My surgeons did a wonderful job both on my surgery and reconstruction, yet was surgery really the right thing to do? It removed the disease, yet absolutely compromised my immune system, which now has to be built up and strengthened.

The more I learn about health and the way our bodies work, especially with alternative "technologies," the more I realize that our bodies were built to self-heal.

We all know that there are two distinct (and usually separated) schools of thought, but did you know that there are also two distinct (and very separated) banks of facts available?

Alternative practitioners usually have the documented medical facts (sadly these are often just the negative ones), whilst the medical practitioners generally have no documented facts or even knowledge of the success rates of alternative treatments.

Hence, often we end up making decisions based on fear because all around us people are fear-oriented. Knowing this, I'm curious as to why I am now learning so much about alternative therapies...after having had surgery!

Maybe God just wanted to reward me with a slim petite body for the journey I am taking!

The important lesson here is that, even if we have compromised, or been compromised (in our health, relationships, financially, or any other way), there must be no regret—just a commitment to help others not to repeat our errors.

My commitment is to continue studying alternatives to invasive surgery so I may coach others on obtaining, and/or keeping, excellent health. All of these "technologies" have incredible testimonials for helping dissipate almost every imaginable disease.

Whether you have already drastically compromised your health or are aware that you may be doing so, I would love to help you.

Meanwhile, remember never to compromise yourself or anyone else intentionally or unintentionally, and if you do (which you will), apologize. And with no regrets, peacefully move on to the next lesson.

What I've learned...

On Magic Moments

I witnessed the most beautiful declaration of love when my dearest cousin created a surprise 60th birthday party for her husband of many years. This was more than just a party—it was an entire magical day, and well worth the trip from Atlanta to New York to participate.

Everything was just perfect, from the beautiful hand-made, personalized invitations (for nearly 70 people!); to organizing rides for those of us who needed them; to an incredible brunch with "surprise guests" (where we ate enough for a week!); to a wonderful walk down the beach where some more "surprise guests" showed up; to the docks where the rest of the "surprise guests" showed up for a wonderful 4-hour cruise with outstanding hors d'oeuvres (where we ate enough for another week); to the music, dancing, singing, guitar-playing, and then a huge selection for dinner (where we ate enough for another week!).

My best discovery was that I have a wonderful extended family that I had never met before, that I can now add to my other wonderful family of friends!

Now getting back to this declaration of love—when was the last time you created a magic moment for someone?

Was it for your spouse, your boy/girlfriend, your parents, or your children?

Was it spontaneous and simple or as complex and committed as the surprise party?

A better question may be: are you open to receiving magic moments?

Creating magic moments for people can take a little effort on our side, yet we can become heroes in the eyes of the receiver.

Be committed to including, and receiving, magic moments in your life—I am!

What I've learned...

On Networking

Summer is here—a time for pool parties, beach parties, birthday parties, picnic parties, and more.

- A time to network with all your friends and have them bring their friends.
- A time to have all the fun you want and to meet all the new people you want.
- A time to write off your party expenses and create legitimate tax deductions...IF you own your own business!

Networking is absolutely the most fun, innovative and cost-effective way of doing business—and you never know who you'll meet.

A few months ago I met a friend of a friend in North Carolina who today put me in touch with his brother in California who just happened to own the gym I used to belong to in Atlanta!

The truth is that what we really network is our reputations and we well know that a poor reputation can spread even faster than a great one.

The way we are being, speaking, connecting, and contributing will reflect on, or deflect off, others very quickly, so it's important to be aware at all times of the energy we are putting out. The stronger our reputation and the higher our standards, the more noticeable it is when we stray.

So party away, network like crazy, be yourself, and keep your light shining. If our lights ever dim, let's be sure and let one another know in a way that will rekindle and not extinguish.

In the words of The Midrash, "Many candles can be kindled from one candle without diminishing it."

What I've learned...

On Celebration

There is nothing like the feeling of celebration and anticipation mixed with gratitude, to get you vibrant enough to attract even bigger and better things. *Excuse Me, Your Life Is Waiting—The Astonishing Power of Feelings* by Lynn Grabhorn is a wonderful book that clearly explains how by focusing on the feelings of celebration, joy, gratitude, and abundance, we will attract more of it.

Now there's the not-so-good-stuff as well—the ex-business partners still not taking care of the commitments, the friends still not paying off their huge debts, etc. However, focusing on their situations of scarcity and guilt (whether consciously or unconsciously) is what brings them more of the same.

Here is a celebration list for you to ponder:

The most destructive habit –*Worry*
The greatest joy –*Giving*
The greatest loss – *Loss of self-respect*
The most satisfying work – *Helping others*
The ugliest personality trait – *Selfishness*
The most endangered species – *Dedicated leaders*
The greatest natural resource – *Our energy*
The greatest "shot in the arm" – *Encouragement*
The greatest problem to overcome – *Fear*
The most effective sleeping pill – *Peace of mind*
The most crippling disease – *Excuses*
The most powerful force in life – *Love*
The most dangerous pariah – *A gossip*
The world's most incredible computer – *The brain*
The worst thing to be without – *Hope*
The deadliest weapon – *The tongue*
The two most power-filled words – *"I can"*
The greatest asset – *Faith*
The most worthless emotion – *Self-pity*
The most beautiful attire – *SMILE!*
The most prized possession – *Integrity*
The most powerful communication channel – *Prayer*
The most contagious spirit – *Enthusiasm*

hat I've learned...

On Gratitude

You want to be motivated?
- Be grateful that you were not at the El Al ticket counter at LAX on July 4th.
- Be grateful that you can sit in a coffee shop with very minimal risk of disturbance.
- Be grateful that you have the ability to read this message.
- Be grateful that you have access to the incredible vehicle called the Internet.

Gratitude is always the very best way for immediate self-motivation!

I am so grateful to my friends who led me to my current home.

Recently the lake area of this subdivision in metro Atlanta was declared a wildlife sanctuary. My home, appropriately named The Sanctuary at Cardinal Lake, is not actually on the lake, yet the local birdies must have heard this declaration and got the word out to their animal friends who decided to make my backyard a wildlife woodland! Even though I am a good mile from the lake, in the last week my backyard has hosted a variety of birds (especially cardinals) squirrels, chipmunks, wild rabbits, a friendly frog, and even a 12-inch turtle. My buried compost even took root and sprouted organic cabbages and a large butternut squash.

Was it the statement of the declaration or was it the power of intention?

We will never know, yet declaring our intention, with strong positive emotion, could be a good indication of how to have our lives work effortlessly, rather than stressfully.

Hmm, something to think about!

hat I've learned...

On September

With children back in school, September is always such a busy month, full of events, high holidays, and celebrations.

- Labor Day, a great time for parties, barbecues, catching up with family and friends, and networking.
- Rosh Hashana—the Jewish New Year.
- The remembrance of 9/11.
- Yom Kippur, the Day of Atonement.

This is probably also an excellent time to remember the prayer of Jabez: "...and Jabez called on the God of Israel and said, 'Oh, that You would bless me indeed and enlarge my territory; that Your hand would be with me, and that You would keep me from evil, that I may not cause pain'—and God granted him what he requested" (I Chronicles 4:9-10).

I wonder which other religions have a full day dedicated to asking God for forgiveness, to be kept from evil, and to cause no pain—I can think of at least one that would benefit!

Meanwhile, know that whatever your religious beliefs, you are being watched over by a higher power and it is for that higher power, and not for us mere mortals, to judge one another. In passing judgment, whether just in our minds or verbally, we can be causing damage far more serious than we may know.

So remember the angels who are up there wanting to connect with us, and this is how you'll know if they are missing you:

I found a penny today, just lying on the ground.
But it's not just a penny, this little coin I've found.
Found pennies come from heaven, that's what my Grandpa told me.
He said Angels toss them down.
He said when an Angel misses you, they toss a penny down.
Sometimes just to cheer you up, to make a smile out of your frown.
So, don't pass by that penny, when you're feeling blue.
It may be a penny from heaven that an Angel's tossed to you.

On Perseverance

Maybe it's the contrasts in life that are the most important.

Maybe without serious disappointment we can't really experience massive success.

Maybe without major health issues we can't really appreciate outstanding health.

Maybe without deep betrayal we can't really understand the blessings of true loyalty.

When I think of the number of times I quit my business over the last 3.5 years, and actually started four other business, none of which succeeded, and all of which cost me a ton of money, either through bad business partners and/or very poor business advice...

When I think of the life and health issues that I had to contend with over the last few years...

I wonder who I would be had I not gone through those lessons...

I wonder if I would have developed the intense gratitude for both my health and financial survival...

Yet from every irritation, whether minor or massive, some people will come—we just need to recognize the pearls in our lives.

This past weekend I received my pearl—the company that I quit several times never quit me. They even awarded me a prestigious gold ring for having earned over $100,000 in a 12-month period on a part-time basis.

The feeling of gratitude (and pride) is overwhelming.

Look around at who, or what, has remained in your life when you may have given them reason to quit, but they stuck around anyway.

Be sure to make them aware of your gratitude.

hat I've learned...

On God's Help

Just when I started to get overwhelmed with projects, the following message arrived from God:

"This is God. Today I will be handling all of your problems for you. I do not need your help. So, have a nice day. I love you. GOD

"P.S. And remember...if life happens to deliver a situation to you that you can not handle, do not attempt to resolve it yourself! Kindly put it in the SFGTD (Something For God To Do) box. I will get to it in My time. All situations will be resolved, but in My time, not yours."

What a relief!

As soon as I placed my situations in the SFGTD box, I immediately felt at peace and was able to concentrate on the more important things in life:

- Writing MMMM when I feel inspired and not just because it's Sunday night.
- Putting on my dancing shoes and dancing until 3 a.m.
- Working with my new excited business associates and loving (from afar) those not yet ready to get excited.
- Working out with my personal trainer and creating some wonderful bicep-tricep definition.
- Taking a limo to and from the airport instead of doing traffic, parking, and heaving bags.
- Getting my kittens neutered, which immediately calmed their temperament and made them more cuddly.
- Crewing yet another Tony Robbins event/firewalk for 270 people and watching their lives transform.
- Seeing the amazing veteran guitarist Les Paul in NYC and being fascinated by his dexterity and humor.

So what is on your mind? What are you working hard to resolve instead of letting it go and having the universe handle it?

In a "bend a spoon with your mind" exercise last week, those who focused their total energy on making a spoon bend were unable to succeed, whilst those who allowed universal energy to come through their bodies had their spoons bend like rubber.

Hmm, something to think about?

hat I've learned...

On Being the Best

"I know it's only rock and roll, but I like, like it, yes I do!"

With hiking the Arizona desert, high-speed motorcycle rides, Las Vegas casinos, dancing the night away, a karaoke dock party with 150 friends, house-boating and speed-boating on Lake Mead, mountain-climbing with coyotes, leadership training on the beach, and a Rolling Stones concert...it's a busy time!

When you work for yourself, and prospecting, recruiting, and training are all a part of your business, life becomes a full-time, tax-deductible adventure!

Jim Rohn, the renowned business philosopher, talks about "Facing the Enemy Within," referring to the self-talk that rules so much of our lives:

- Indifference: why bother seeking new adventures, I'm comfortable in my nice home.
- Indecision: there are too many choices, which one adventure should I choose?
- Doubt: these are all new experiences—what if I mess up?
- Worry: how could I possibly enjoy myself with all the challenges I currently have in my life?
- Timidity: what if I decide to go and no-one wants to play with me?

We have all asked ourselves questions like these. The sad truth is that this just limits our life experiences.

Why not be all you can be, do all you can do, have all you can have, and help as many people as possible along the way?

The late Audrey Hepburn had the best way of expressing this and we would all do well to remember and practice these exercises:

For attractive lips, speak words of kindness.

For lovely eyes, seek out the good in people.

For beautiful hair, let a child run his/her fingers through it once a day.

For poise, walk with the knowledge that you never walk alone

On Relationships

Relationships—oh, what a complex subject!

Whether they be family relationships, business relationships, friendships, or intimate relationships, if we ultimately all want the same things (peace, happiness, joy, abundance, fulfillment), why is it such a challenge to stay in a harmonious relationship?

I find it curious that there are so many wonderful single individua looking for their life partners, yet such a small percentage are actually hooking up.

Truly the first step must be to take time out alone and get in relationship with oneself; if we can't get along with ourselves, how can w possibly expect others to get along with us?

The second step came to me in an epiphany, with the realization that we usually focus on what went wrong in a relationship so as not to repeat the errors. I decided instead to take inventory of the very best attributes that each of my previous partners had brought to the respective relationships so as to truly design the ultimate partner. It was amazing ho many great attributes I found: abundance, caring, decisiveness, empathy, passion, practicality, sexiness, vision. How blessed I have been.

So let's count our blessings, know that the future is exciting, and from now on, let's make a commitment just to focus on the positive side (life.

You may be only one person in the world, but you may also be the world to one person!

Happiness comes through doors you didn't even know you left open!

Some mistakes are too much fun to only make once!

Don't cry because it's over; smile because it happened!

Birthdays are good for you; the more you have, the longer you live!

A truly happy person is one who can enjoy the scenery on a detour!

Living on earth is expensive, but it does include a free trip around the sun every year!

Ever notice that the people who are late are often much jollier than the people who have to wait for them!

What I've learned...

On Laughter

How often do you laugh, I mean really laugh?

True laughter is such a healer, yet many of us either don't laugh enough or laugh at another's misfortune or laugh (hysterically) at everything whether things are funny or not! Then, of course, there are those special people who have learned to laugh at themselves (the hardest thing to do when ego is still present).

If it's true, and it is, that we become like the people we spend the most time with, then let's start paying very close attention. Take a moment and write down the names of the five people you are in communication with the most, whether in person or on the phone (email doesn't really count for this exercise).

Then ask yourself:

- Do they laugh often and from the heart?
- Are they in touch with their spirit or their ego?
- Do they take care of their physical bodies?
- Are they abundant in thought and deed?
- Do they truly enjoy both giving and receiving from the heart?
- Are they truly listening to you?
- Do they stay in touch because they love you or because the need you?

This is an eye-opening exercise if you are truthful with yourself.

If you don't laugh enough, then try this exercise with your family or at your next party:

Lie down on the floor, have the next person lie down with their head on your belly, the third has their head on the second person' belly, etc., until you have a chain of people around the room. The first person says "ha," the second one says "ha, ha," the third one says "ha, ha, ha," etc. and you will all end up laughing so hard that your sides will ache!

If the thought of lying down on the floor with strangers is too much, you can get a joke book instead!

On Tolerations

"Amazed in America."

As I ponder over the events of the last few years, I realize how often we filter and sugar-coat situations in order to continue to accept them versus making a decision to eliminate them. In retrospect, when looking at many of these situations, especially the ones related to how th American "system" works, I am constantly amazed.

When the Kudzu vine started taking over the woodland in my backyard, it became a wonderful metaphor for some of the weeds growin in my personal life. Interestingly enough, it also coincided with visits fro a couple of individuals whom I had allowed in the past to choke up my li garden.

For years I had been tolerating certain situations and people in m life, knowing that their behavior and, worst still, my acceptance of that behavior, was wrong. Yet I was afraid to recognize it as the truth in case I really had to take drastic action...and we all know that change hurts!

We all have weeds in our lives and, sometimes, they actually flower—then we get confused and forget what (who) they really are. Think carefully now and pay attention to the ones that may be confusing you!

It is time to take action, draw a line in the sand, say no (when it's much easier to say yes), and stand for the truth and nothing but the truth. They say the truth will never harm us, yet it takes a lot of faith. So let thi week's focus be on strengthening your faith.

hat I've learned...

On Unconditional Love

Mothering Sunday is always a reminder for us to look at the commitments we made as a mother and ask ourselves if we are always demonstrating unconditional love.

How many of us parents sometimes find it easier to judge than to love unconditionally?

How often do we take the good behavior for granted, yet criticize our children when they get off track?

Why is it so much easier to acknowledge our colleagues and friends than it is to praise our loved ones?

It's hard to understand the balance between being non-judgmental and having expectations for people to fulfill their commitments.

We have such faith and caring for our family, friends, and colleagues that we often get caught up in really believing something will change.

The definition of insanity is "doing the same thing and expecting things to change."

Sometimes it's just time to move on, find a coach, create a new peer group, look for new mentors—and take life to the next level!

I encourage you to continually review who and what is in your life and make the necessary adjustments.

Just remember that your children will always remain your children no matter what, so love them every day, in every way.

On Kittens

Want to increase your abundance quotient? Increase your gratitude—and practice it at every opportunity.

Want to increase your health quotient? Alkalize your body—eat organic vegetables and sprouts and drink lots of greens.

Want to increase your unconditional love quotient? Get a pet—of the non-human kind!

Want to increase your laughter quotient? Get a pair of kittens and camera!

Recently I became a first-time "kitty-mama" and adopted two 8-week old kittens, Zahav and Hayim (Hebrew for "Gold" and "Life").

Luring them out of their box (with some fresh grilled salmon!), watching them venture out and start to explore, listening to them calling one another as they discovered new hiding places, guiding them to their food and water and kitty litter...what a trip!

Within a matter of hours they were eating solid foods, fully potty trained, familiar with two stories of the house, leaping all over the furniture, chasing each other's tails, fighting one minute and licking each other's faces to make up the next, and generally behaving extremely independently.

Oh, that we could learn in a decade or two what kittens can learn a day!

The simple pleasures of curling up and napping when we're tired, basking in direct sunlight, face-licking (OK...kissing) at every opportunity, covering up (i.e. closing the toilet seat) after using the potty, and communicating verbally so that we really understand one another.

What a peaceful, playful, and fun life that would be. So commit to behaving like a kitten—together we can "take the world and make it a better place."

On Luxury

Nothing motivates us to work hard like needing to cover the necessities in life—of course, some of the things we feel are necessary, may seem like luxuries to others.

A gardener to mow the lawn, a cleaner to do the house, a bookkeeper to pay the bills, a son who has just decided to go to an Ivy League school—necessities or luxuries?

Recently I misplaced my day-timer with all the details of my family, friends, and business associates—phone numbers, appointments, financial statements, tax returns (not yet submitted), and more.

Many kind friends pointed out that there must be a lesson to learn in this (yes, I do know that...and have looked hard for the lesson in missing previously booked appointments!).

Many kind friends reminded me, "If you visualize it strongly enough, it will show up." (I had the image of my day-timer firmly implanted in my brain for over 2 weeks—it still didn't show up!)

So what does this have to do with necessities versus luxuries?

The most important lesson that came out of this was the commitment to use leverage. Recreating all the lost data will take a lot of time—leveraging out some of the work (i.e. redoing tax returns) and other tasks that don't leave me fulfilled (i.e. house cleaning, lawn mowing), gives me the time to recreate some of the lost data.

Once this is done, by continuing to leverage out these tasks, I can focus on building my health, my business, and my relationships—areas for which I have a true passion.

Are you using leverage in your life?

Are there areas where you spend a considerable amount of time that do not leave you fulfilled or at least reward you well financially?

Take a moment to see where you are spending your time and what you can leverage or trade with others.

It's time to realize that life is meant to be fun and abundant, so be sure to make the choices that will lead you there!

On Easter/Passover

Easter 2002 brought with it the passing of England's wonderful Queen Mother—what a matriarch (and I remember thinking she was really old when I was in kindergarten, many decades ago!).

Passover brought with it five suicide bombings throughout Israel in as many days—what an incredible tragedy.

Jim Rohn says it best in his comment, "The challenge of leadership is to be strong, but not rude; be kind, but not weak; be bold, but not a bully; be thoughtful, but not lazy; be humble, but not timid; be proud, but not arrogant; have humor, but without folly." Oh, that our countries' leaders would follow those guidelines.

Where does the solution lie in the Middle East where two peoples live on the same land with such vastly conflicting values? If it is wrong that the Israelis should use such force in oppressing the Palestinian uprising (albeit making every effort to remove the militant leaders and avoid harming innocent civilians), then is it not terribly wrong that suicide bombers should go into the most crowded areas for their missions (to ensure the maximum numbers of civilian deaths and casualties)?

However, we must always remember that things work out best for the people who make the most of how things work out!

This is a time for self awareness, remembering that the most important opinion in the world is the one you hold of yourself.

This is a time for faith and forgiveness, a time for prayers and peace, a time for light and love.

On Jabez

"Mama...Dada." We waited expectantly for my son's first word over two decades ago, yet the first word was "more"! (I guess that's why he grew so tall and has such a zest for life!)

The prayer of Jabez suggests we ask for more:

- The more we give, the more we get.
- The more we ask for, the more we get.
- The more we do, the more results we get.
- The more we take (nurture ourselves), the more we have to give.

Sounds like abundance to me!

When we give more listening to those who need to talk, more words of encouragement to those who are down, more financial contribution to those in need, what do we get? More surprise gifts, more special deals, and more opportunities!

The challenge is that there's always more—more that we can be, have, and do. The key is to discover the balance between business and life, to make sure we are getting all our needs filled—getting enough gre nutrition, exercise, rest, work, money, family time, relaxation, relationships, sex, social/cultural time, etc.

You may be reading this and agreeing with it all, but it's what you do with this information that counts!

Who loses weight? The one who knows all about the benefits of exercise or the one who walks 3 miles a day?

Who makes the most sales? The one who believes they can become a great salesperson or the one who makes 10 sales calls a day?

Who retires early? The one who dreams of a house on the beach the one who invests $300 a month?

Who writes books? The one who desires to become a best-selling author or the one who gets up early and writes for half an hour per day?

Who has the best marital relationship? The one who knows how much spending time with their spouse can improve their relationship or the one who sits down and talks with their spouse every night?

Commit to more—getting and giving more—and make your life masterpiece.

On Strategies

The way we handle situations depends on two things—the minds we are in at that time and our previous references for similar situations.

There are two main ways to achieve our outcome with other people:

1) we can create rapport and connection to find out what motivates the other person and get there with pleasure, or
2) we can take a short cut and find our strongest leverage, and g our outcome by inflicting pain.

How many times has some unwitting individual felt the brunt of our emotions because we used past references that had nothing to do wit this specific situation?

The best strategy is always to try pleasure first, by treating the other party as if there was a misunderstanding on our side, and not by holding them at fault.

Only when this doesn't work should we consider strategy numbe two.

However, remember the prayer of Jabez? And Jabez called on the God of Israel, 'Oh Lord, that You would bless me indeed, and enlarge my territory; that Your hand would be with me; and that You would keep me from evil; that I may not cause pain.' And God granted him what he requested" (I Chronicles 4:9-10).

Strangely enough, that wish to "cause no pain" can actually take away from our ability to do the right thing—sometimes using leverage (a.k.a. pain) with others is the only way to come to completion.

Being okay with the second strategy required that I reframe my interpretation. When you promise and do not do, I feel pain. When I do nothing to help you keep your promise, I feel more pain.

God does not want us to cause pain for others and especially not cause pain to ourselves.

Therefore, to avoid causing immeasurable pain to me, I may nee to inflict some pain on you!

Here's to doing the right thing the first time around and focusing on the pleasure at all times!

What I've learned...

On Purpose

Which way are you going: towards the light or away from the light?

If you are headed in the wrong direction anyway, don't worry, God won't bother you.

If you are headed in the right direction, watch out! God will help strengthen you on your path. How? By sending more and more (and more "stuff" your way.

So as my week piled up with more "stuff" than I ever thought possible that one person should be expected to handle, I called to God for help, which led me back to my faith, which led me to call some trusted friends, which led me to gratitude for some very wonderful people I have in my life.

In 24 hours it is possible to go the full circle, from fear and desperation all the way through to love and gratitude.

We've heard that God will not give us more challenges than we can handle, but, if you're anything like me, every now and again you may ask, "Why me?"

Les Brown asks a better question: "Why NOT you? Who would you rather this happens to?"

Now, before you come up with some names to answer this question, think it through: do you really want someone else to do your work? Will making it easy for you really make you stronger?

Remember your purpose and the path will open up.

hat I've learned...

On Fathers

Father's Day is the time to think about our fathers and acknowled them for giving us life, even if they are no longer in our lives today. Som of us lost our fathers through old age, ill health, or accidents. Others lost their fathers when they took a different course and decided to no longer part of the family unit.

This is the time to count your blessings if your father is still in yo life, especially if you have a wonderful and supportive relationship.

This is the time to recall all the wonderful things we learned from our fathers, even though the lessons may have been tough, disciplined, o communicated in an uninspiring way.

For those of you who are fathers, and still living with or in great relationship with your children, blessings to you.

For those of you who are fathers and not in contact with, or in denial of, your children, this is a time for reflection. Understand just how much your children need you in their lives, even if you cannot give them 100% of you, give them what you can, and listen to the song "Butterfly Kisses" to understand just how much that will mean to them.

For those of you, mothers or fathers, who are acting the role and carrying the burden, of both parents, this is the time to forgive the one w left and count your blessings that you have your children with you.

Find a father to acknowledge today and acknowledge him in person. You will make two people very happy and the world will be a much better place for your efforts.

hat I've learned...

On Collaboration

How on earth did we get so busy with so much technology available to help us?

Many of us are trying to do it all—be all things to all people—and it just can't be done.

The key is collaboration.

With collaboration, we get amazing leverage by using everyone's strengths on a project—never having to do things we don't do well, because someone else can do them better!

With collaboration, we can put the balance back in our lives— check out this great metaphor by an ex-CEO of a major corporation:

> Imagine life is a game in which you are juggling five balls in the air. You can name them—work, family, health, friends, and spirit—and you are keeping all of these in the air. You will soon understand that work is a rubber ball. If you drop it, it'll bounce back. The other balls—family, health, friends, and spirit—are made of glass. If you drop one of these, it will be irrevocably scuffed, marked, nicked, damaged, or even shattered. They'll never be the same and you must understand that and strive for balance in your life.

To balance your family—commit to exclusive family time every week (preferably, daily).

To balance your health—commit to plenty of organic vegetables and fruits and a daily exercise routine.

To balance your friends—commit to weekly social time, but only with those who support your purpose and inspire you.

To balance your spirits—dance in an IHOP parking lot on a Monday morning!

With collaboration, I decided to publish my first book, *Monday Morning Motivational Moments*. Within a few short weeks of that decision, the book was complete!

On Revolution

The New Year's Revolution has begun—time to revolt and to get rid of the "revolting" stuff in your life!

We all make New Year's resolutions as we resolve to take action in the upcoming year—the revolution is when we take action!

We look at what's happening in our lives and resolve to change what is not working—the revolution means we change it.

We look at our health habits, diets, and exercise programs and resolve to change them—the revolution means eating right and working out today.

We look at the people we care about and how we let them off the hook because we care—the revolution means caring for them by holding them accountable.

We look at our relationships, who is there for us no matter what, versus who is not, and resolve to better define them—the revolution mea defining and sticking only by the relationships that support us.

I challenge you to start the revolution in your life today and I look forward to hearing from you at the end of the year as to how your revolution has taken your life to a whole new level!

On Lessons

As the end of the year draws nigh, it's time to reflect on everythin we have learned this year.

As I sat in a workshop recently, the facilitator asked, "Where wer you a year ago, and how far have you come this year?"

My original thought was that this has been one heck of a tough year—a son on active duty in a war zone, a daughter struggling through personal challenges and moving overseas, personal major health issues and surgery with huge financial implications.

Then I took a moment and reflected what this year has really meant and the blessings it has brought:

- I've learned that people are at different stages of development in different areas of their life—mature in business yet immature financially, mature in health habit yet immature in relationships.
- I've learned that if we buy into traditional methods of healing and normal healing times, that's what we'll get; alternatively we can believe in accelerated healing and we get miracles.
- I've learned that when we really love something about somebody, we'll overlook the weaknesses just to keep the bits that we love.
- I've learned that God and nature provide us with everythi we need to heal, and we cannot improve on nature's living foods.
- I've learned how changing one's thinking from fear and scarcity to faith and abundance will help us through everything.
- I've learned that we can never have too many friends and can never help one another too much.
- I've learned that sometimes we need to separate from tho we love so that we can both heal.
- I've learned to ask for help and trade services instead of thinking I have to do it all myself.
- I've learned that healing happens from the inside out, not from the outside in.

- I've learned that physical scars do not change sexy, but emotional scars can.
- I've learned that faith, love, and health are the only things truly worth having.
- I've learned that I don't need to do this year over again!

How many of these lessons have you learned? And what lessons d blessings await you in the coming year?

---

hat I've learned...

WHAT I'VE LEARNED

And now, for what I've really learned:

If you're too open minded, your brains will fall out!

Age is a very high price to pay for maturity!

Going to church doesn't make you a Christian any more than going to a garage makes you a mechanic!

Artificial intelligence is no match for natural stupidity!

If you must choose between two evils, pick the one you've never tried before!

My idea of housework is to sweep the room with a glance!

Not one shred of evidence supports the notion that life is serious!

It is easier to get forgiveness than permission!

For every action, there is an equal and opposite government program!

If you don't look like your passport picture, you probably nee the trip!

Bills travel through the mail at twice the speed of checks!

A conscience is what hurts when all your other parts feel so good!

Eat well, stay fit, die anyway!

Men are from earth. Women are from earth. Deal with it!

No husband has ever been shot while doing the dishes!

A balanced diet is a cookie in each hand!

Middle age is when broadness of the mind and narrowness o the waist change places!

Opportunities always look bigger going than coming!

Junk is something you've kept for years and thrown away three weeks before you need it!

There is always one more imbecile than you counted on!

Experience is a wonderful thing. It enables you to recognize a mistake when you make it again!

By the time you can make ends meet, they move the ends!

Someone who thinks logically provides a nice contrast to the real world!

Blessed are they who can laugh at themselves...for they shall never cease to be amused!

And finally:

An Oyster's Tale

There once was an oyster whose story I tell,
Who found that some sand had got into his shell.
It was only a grain, but it gave him great pain.
For oysters have feelings although they're so plain.
Now, did he berate the harsh workings of fate
That had brought him to such a deplorable state?
Did he curse at the government, cry for election,
And claim that the sea should have given him protection?
'No,' he said to himself as he lay on a shell,
Since I cannot remove it, I shall try to improve it.
Now the years have rolled around, as years always do,
And he came to his ultimate destiny; stew,
And the small grain of sand that had bothered him so
Was a beautiful pearl all richly aglow.
Now the tale has a moral, for isn't it grand
What an oyster can do with a morsel of sand?
What couldn't we do if we'd only begin
With some of the things that get under our skin.

What I've learned...

PRAISE FOR *MONDAY MORNING MOTIVATIONAL MOMENTS*

"An absolutely extraordinary array of motivational and inspirational high points that will begin your day with a charging bang! I this is not the perfect "morning coffee," then I certainly don't know what is!" *–Mike Litman, Radio personality, #1 Best-selling author* Conversations with Millionaires, *New York, NY*

"Linda's *(Monday Morning Motivational Moments)* kiss-start the week with love, joy, creativity, and passion. A week well-started is a week well-lived." *–Judy May Murphy, TV lifecoach, author of* That Girl from Happy *and* Your Life Only a Gazillion Times Better, *Ireland*

"One of the few e-zines I make sure to read without fail. Each and every issue is filled with nuggets of wisdom-filled gold, as it relates to people's lives financially, emotionally, and spiritually. She not only talks the talk, but walks it. You'll be richer for it." *–Bob Burg, author of* Endles Referrals *and* Winning Without Intimidation, *Jupiter, FL*

"Linda is the most dynamic and inspirational woman I know. She knows life and how to live it to the fullest. This book is an absolute must read for those who want to get every drop out of life." *–David Baulieu, business owner and professional entrepreneur, Huntersville, NC*

"My spirits always lighten a little when I open my email and see that the Monday Morning Motivational Moments message is there waitir for me. Linda's mix of just the right amount of humor and good advice helps me start the week off in the right frame of mind." *–Shari Powell, Owner of Sharpp Data Management, Inc., Atlanta, GA*

"Thank you for all of the Monday motivations. Linda has so muc to offer this world. She has inspired me so much." *–Lisa Lockwood, Narcotics detective, Chicago, IL*

"I read the MMMM's because they are so uplifting and inspiring a little encouraging push on Monday morning to make it even a better week. I am so grateful to Linda, she is a great role model for me. I hope e will continue to write for a long, long time." *–Ann Marie Smulders, terior designer, The Hague, Holland*

"Linda's *(Monday Morning Motivational Moments)* is THE best ay to start your week. No matter how I feel when I wake up every [onday morning, Linda's MMMMs inspire and motivate me to take ntrol of my day and my life." *–Erika Z. Muelle, Internet consultant and esident of EZM Enterprises, Inc., Manhattan Beach, CA*

"Ms. Kedy can always be counted on for an uplifting message. I ok forward to receiving her weekly newsletter and we are all fortunate d blessed to have her spirit and comments in a book!" *–Carole Madan .k.a. Momma Nature), Founder of the Alpharetta Writers Club, author d award-winning poet, Atlanta, GA*

"Statistics show that Monday mornings are the most stressful nes, filled with anxiety about the week ahead. Life, our successes, our lfillment, our health, our relationship with ourselves and others, is really out the choices we make. Linda's Monday Morning Motivational oments come at a time when we need it most—Monday mornings—and lp me to focus on all that I have to be thankful for and help me make a nscious decision to be happy.

"Linda is a master motivator and her insight, from years of battling e odds, would benefit anyone who wants to break free, realize his or her ll potential, and enjoy all that life has to offer." *–Jean Tenuta, ealthcare consultant, author, entrepreneur, Kenosha, WI*

"Linda Kedy's words have the happy knack of touching and lifting ur soul. Of a Monday morning her words are the first I read, and, ithout fail, they are relevant and make me smile. Buy this book and u'll benefit from her warmth, wisdom, and infectious, fun-loving spirit." *Niamh Hooper, Journalist, Irish Independent*

"Linda shares her most vulnerable wisdom that has transformed r life through beautifully touching, heart-felt stories. Her work both allenges and encourages readers to look deeper within themselves so at they, too, may experience greater peace in their lives. I've personally en inspired and am delighted that she's organized the most influential ticles into a book that can affect even more lives." *–Mary Allen, CPCC, fe coach, Laguna Beach, CA*

SPECIAL ACKNOWLEDGMENTS

With acknowledgement and thanks to all of the following owners of the first-run limited edition version of *Monday Morning Motivational Moments*:

Marsha Lewis, Jesse Kedy, Les & Kate Billig, Kayli Covington, Jerry Goldman, David Billig, Ruth & Dani Drori, Maureen Mack, Keith Leeson, Paul J Meyer, Vince Petrell, Rae Jensan, Henry Brent, Jeannie Austin, Carol Polokoff, Beth Komisar, Rebecca Friedrick, Stephen Mayer, Dr Steve Sherman, Arvin Thomas, Amber Dotts, Jaime Howard, John Burgess, Amie Lee Marks, Dr Maite Casanova, Dr Amy Creech, Dr George Kostakis, Dr Sandy L'Amie, John (Woody) Marks, Lisa Lockwood, Louie Pinto, Alison Gruhler, Dave Mirabito, Lorna Rasmussen, Lucretia Daniel, Linda Rasmussen, Marie Fratoni, Nanette Freiman, Jackie Walters, Jean Tenuta, Erica Zacarias, Jane Royal, Bob Lamp'l, Michelle Henderson, Barbara Becker, Ane Whaling, Kathleen Christman, Bob Burg, Miki Bell, Lee Ring, Maria Siebald, Paula Shlora, Dr John Gray, Anne Hallewell, Chris & Mary Hill, Brian Mast, Robert Scott Bell, Suka, Laura Roth-Shepherd, Loren Slocum, Dr Traci Mosher, Pamela Taylor, Bob Levy, Carolyn Fessenden, Darlene Malz, Karen Bershad, Beth Howison, Dr Hug Fouasse, Mimi Gabriel, Jack Tann, Katherine Rourke, Cynthia Stewart, Robert Wadley, Regina Jimison, Wayne Pulkin, Margaret Irving, Mary Allen, Andy Bailey, Michele Lasy, Orrin Hudson, Eunice Carter, Judy Sutter, Mark Victor Hansen, Carole Gardner, Sahara Russell, John Eagle, Wayne Heard, Carole Grove, Rick Campbell, Belinda Eckard, Imani & Ativa Davis, Dr Mark Barr, Denise Taddonio, Cindy Alena, Jacqui Taylor, Blanca Villasenor, Jere Shahid, Mimma Mancuso, David & Cherelle Stecki, Rodney & Tao Summerville, Adrian Drost, Darinda Teeling, John Mulkey, Lenald & JaeHae Burgess, Dolly Martinez, Sonny Kane, Bill Keefe, Lawrence Garrett, Ron & Nancy Sweet, Delon Henegar, Anne-Marie Smulders, Judy-May Murphy, Marjan Drost, Mary Stripling, Carol Madan, Susan Roberts, Sean Metcalfe, Margo Fallis, Paul Cossman, Dr Kathleen Byers-Lindsey, Kathleen

Boehmig, Kathleen Mainland, Dr Deborah Forrest, Penny Holder, Elizabeth Vargus, Carolyn Lewis, Jose Rodriguez, Lee Mays, Greg White, Alfred Duncan, James Cousins, Yvonne & Harvey Mathis, Terry Barfield, Feroz Penangwala, April Dubois, Dr Hazel Du Bois, Judy Gaicomozzi, Trenell Smith, Thomas Searles, Kevin Mack, Christian Rogner, Fred Duff, Jeff Olson, Robert Adler, Nick Serba, Andrea Rodriguez, Janet & Arnie Sohns, Keith Davis, Nancy Boetto, Tonya & Tony Petrill, Bobbie Kugeler, Jim Kugeler, Joyce Herndon, Jimmy Santos, Kate A'Vard, Bill Carter, Linda Diesel, Ellen Reach, Kathy Holdaway, Judy Osuna, Bonnie Lindberg, Sonya Rierson, Susan Alley, Linda Zobel, Elizabeth Braun, Danny Driggers, Tad & Jeanna Smith, Betty Nobles, Mart Patrick, Robert Tallent, Gladys Grier, Jilian Saweczko, Carol Lommen, Chris Clausen, John Joyce, James & Sherry Sanford, Linda-Jo Beckers, Karen Tindal, Cheryl Capitani, Terry Potter, Darien Norman, Cindy Wright, Phyllis Zitzer, Jacob Samuel, William Dean, Mark Williams, Victoria Varela, and Socheat Chea.

Thank you from the bottom of my heart for your ongoing
ɲport!

Linda

UNLOCKING YOUR LEGACY
25 KEYS FOR SUCCESS

FOREWORD BY
JOHN C. MAXWELL

UNLOCKING
YOUR
LEGACY

25
KEYS FOR
SUCCESS

PAUL J. MEYER

NEW YORK TIMES BEST SELLING AUTHOR

UNLOCKING
YOUR
LEGACY
25 KEYS FOR SUCCESS
BY PAUL J. MEYER

Part One:
WHERE EVERY
GOOD LEGACY
BEGINS

Disc One

1. DEDICATION AND INTRODUCTION
2. LEGACY KEY #1 — LOVE — WHERE EVERY GOOD LEGACY BEGINS
3. LEGACY KEY #2 — WE ALL STAND ON LEVEL GROUND
4. LEGACY KEY #3 — TELLING OTHERS ABOUT YOUR FAITH
5. LEGACY KEY #4 — THE JOURNEY OF PRAYER

℗ 2002 Paul J. Meyer
ALL RIGHTS RESERVED
PJM10216

Learn How To
LIVE YOUR LIFE WITH YOUR FUTURE IN MIND...

When all is said and done each of us will leave only 4 things behind. Paul J. Meyer tells you what these are and how they affect your legacy!

Available on CD

"As you read Paul's wisdom, advice, and personal stories, keep in mind that he has already done what he is talking about. He isn't talking theory — he's talking reality!"

—From the Foreword by
JOHN C. MAXWELL

"If you have a thousand books in your library and don't have this book, consider your library empty! This book is a must."

—**KEN BLANCHARD**
Co-author, The One Minute Manager

MORE MUST READ TITLES
from Paul J. Meyer Resources

The Five Pillars of Leadership

The Leadership Gap presents a shortage of leaders who successfully integrate their lives with their work. Learn how to change all that with the help of leadership specialists Paul J. Meyer and Randy Slechta. *(paperback)*

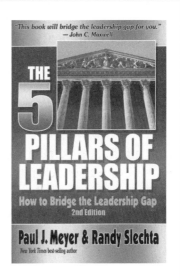

"This book will bridge the leadership gap for you."
— John C. Maxwell

THE
5
PILLARS OF
LEADERSHIP
How to Bridge the Leadership Gap
2nd Edition

Paul J. Meyer & Randy Slechta
New York Times best-selling author

The Art of Giving

Most people think giving is a luxury they can't afford, but Paul J. Meyer is a role model who shows that isn't true. He doesn't give his surplus earnings; he sets giving targets, then works to meet them. John Edmund Haggai writes this remarkable story! *(paperback)*

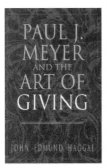

PAUL J. MEYER AND THE ART OF GIVING

JOHN EDMUND HAGGAI

I Inherited a FORTUNE!

Ideas for empowering you with your own "fortune" can be found in this compelling book. These warm remembrances from the remarkable life and career of Paul J. Meyer are not only lessons in living, they are studies in success. *(paperback)*

PAUL J. MEYER

I Inherited a FORTUNE!

SAVINGS UP TO 50% OFF RETAIL!
By Ordering These & Other Great Books, CDs, & Cassettes From
PAUL J. MEYER RESOURCES
Online: **www.pauljmeyer.com** • Toll free **1-888-750-4811**

For information on having Linda as your personal life coach and for your free Life Balance evaluation, visit: www.HealThySpirits.com or email Linda@HealThySpirits.com

To order additional copies of *Monday Morning Motivational Moments* and find out about special quantity discounts, visit: www.MondayMotivations.com or email Orders@MondayMotivations.com.

For information on the opportunity to work with Linda and start your own home-based business, visit: www.LindaKedy.net or email Linda@MondayMotivations.com.